From a Handful of
ASHES

Elke Kaiser Carrihill

From a Handful of Ashes

Published by Elke Kaiser Carrihill

Winterton, 3340

ecarrihill@nelcsa.net

ISBN 978-0-7961-3131-7

eISBN 978-0-7961-3121-4

2 4 6 8 10 9 7 5 3 1

Layout and cover design by Boutique Books

Printed in South Africa

From a Handful of
ASHES

Foreword

I have known Elke Kaiser Carrihill for over 28 years, since our days in the late 1990s studying theology together in Pietermaritzburg, South Africa. In the last few years, our paths have crossed again. Things had changed and so had we changed.

Basking in the glory of being crowned 2023 Rugby World Champions, allow me to use the expression of the captain of the Springboks. For me, being asked by Elke to write a few words as an introduction to this work: This is not pressure; it is a privilege and an honour.

It was during these last few years Elke would share with me her creative passion for poetry. I immediately recognised a gift that she had been blessed with. Reflecting on the beauty of the words she penned, I was in awe and asked myself: Is this the Elke I know? Where does this come from?

This morning at prayer a scriptural refrain from Matthew's Gospel came to mind: "It won't be you speaking but the Spirit of your Father speaking through you". This captures something of the words of life that you will read in *From a Handful of Ashes*. Perhaps Elke's calling as a Lutheran pastor and her life's journey have contributed to this work of God. It is deeply personal, yet also an expression of the cultural and political realities of the day in South Africa and beyond.

I particularly loved the question posed to Barabbas: "What did you do with your freedom?" I used this poem for a sermon during the liturgical season of Lent last year. There are so many challenging and yet hope-filled moments in the reading of these poems.

Bless you, Elke, in sharing this gift with others, as it will bring much peace and hope to many needing someone to speak for them.

In gratitude.
Peter Foley

Dedication

For my son David, my parents, my family and to friends.

And
I dedicate this book to the brave men and women
Whom I have been privileged to meet
Men and Women
Who have faced life with courage
Who have walked into the broken pieces of this world
And brought light into dark places

I dedicate it to those
Who have faced their own shadows
Who have not shied away
But took on their inner struggles
With fear, guilt, shame and pain
With courage and faith

I dedicate these lines
To unfinished stories
To messy lives
To fearful souls
To broken hearts
To courage and hope
To deeper meaning
To age old wisdom
To Faith – To Hope – To Love

I dedicate these words
To the many faces
Who have inspired and taught me
How to write life's colourful story –
From a handful of Ashes

How this booklet came about

On 9 July 2021, our country woke up to a spate of violent looting in Kwazulu-Natal. I remember the peaceful night I had had – only to wake up to my little world and my ideologies of our country being turned on its head. All over social media, the news, the radio – everywhere, all we heard were reports of violent looting that had erupted around us. Buildings were burning, people were smashing windows of shops and helping themselves to whatever they could carry, and there was a strange noise that overtook our country that day.

I remember these days clearly – but most of all I remember trying to make sense of what was unfolding in our country. It was in this time that all I knew to do was to "put pen to paper" and somehow try to express and create order in my messy mind and my hurting heart.

It was here that my love for writing poetry was born. After the violence and the noise had died down, I experienced many moments when this need to put into words and order my thoughts and feelings overcame me. So, I continued to write. Searching for words and deeper meaning, often midst rubble and despair.

This little booklet is a compilation of some of these processes. Often the words were born from pain and despair, anxiety and confusion. When I reflected on the title of the book, it was one poems title that summed it up: From a handful of ashes!

Many times, it feels like we hold very little in our hands, but a handful of ashes. Many times life, our country, our world seem hopeless and leave us speechless. BUT THEN, if we look closely, we will find there is always a message in the mess. We need to look closely and sometimes from a different angle – but I believe that there is nearly always something to be learned "from a handful of ashes".

Thank you to all who inspired me through this process. Thank you to friends and family who cheered me on. Thank you to my nephew Ruben Dedekind, who put some of these words into drawings.

I hope you find some courage, some meaning, hope, inspiration, comfort and some peace as you read these pages, written simply: **From a hand full of ashes**.

Contents

FOR OUR COUNTRY
– SOUTH AFRICA

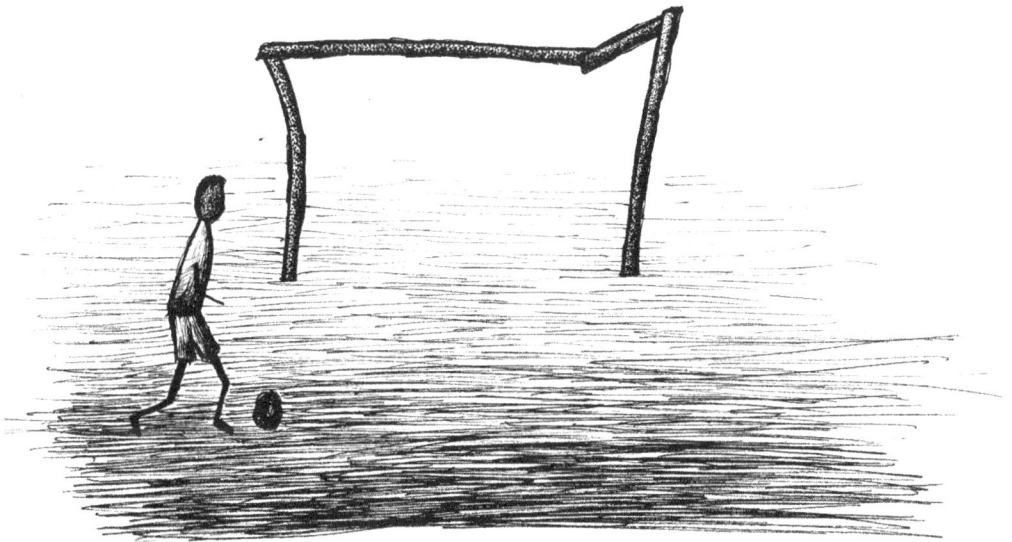

Cry – the beloved country

After the last couple of days I have watched and listened as violent protestors have taken to the streets of our country. My mind has been a jumble of thoughts, trying to make sense of what is happening in our "beloved country". Continuously it was the title of Alan Paton's book (written in 1946) that echoes through the ever thickening and paralysing cloud of smoke that has descended on me:

"Cry, the beloved country".

Through the fog of my mind, I try and hear the emotions of my soul –
It is this: CRY – the beloved country.
Cry – for broken lives and unmet dreams;
Cry – for silent voices and uncontrolled rage;
Cry – for hearts of greed and empty hands;
Cry – for fists of violence and fear-filled souls;
Cry – for hope-filled courage and courage that has lost hope;

And through the fog and my paralysed being –
Through the words of Paton's title –
There is BUT just one verse that makes its way through:
"JESUS WEPT".

(Written July 2021)

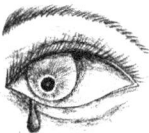

For you: our beautiful Rainbow!

South Africa – our Rainbow has been covered;
Covered in a dark cloud of dust and smoke!
For now, we cannot see you –
Your beautiful colours are barely visible,
behind the different shades of darkness.
But know that behind the shades of grey
the colours are still there;
Behind the smoke and the rubble, WE are there –
A people of UBUNTU
People of: "I am because you are".
People who reach out and cares for their neighbour –
People who rally together when hardship strikes –
People who reach out with hands of compassion and
    kindness –
People who laugh together and hold each other in grief –
People who wants a beautiful future for all!

For now, we may seem hidden behind this dark cloud
But we are still here –
Yes – covered in dust and ashes
Yes – standing midst rubble and a shattered existence;
BUT WE ARE STILL **HERE!**

And when the dust and ash has settled
We will rise, and we will clean, and we will restore.
We will polish you so that you can shine again;
We will wipe away the remnants of dust that continue to
    cover you;

We will put our hearts and souls to work
to restore the broken places on your bruised contours;
We will rise with our hearts of UBUNTU –
And we will courageously and peacefully work,
Hand in hand

FOR YOU: OUR BEAUTIFUL RAINBOW.

One stitch at a time

South Africa:
In the last week, our fragile existence has been laid bare.
The threads that have barely held together the thin worn
    fabric of our country
Have finally ripped apart!
We stand exposed to that which lay underneath,
From whatever angle we look at it:
Be it politics, economics, societal structures, or theology;
Be it criminality, lawlessness, corruption, racism, poverty or
    inequality.
Be it all of the above and so much more,
The already thin worn fabric has been ripped apart.

And now the frayed edges lie at our feet.
Where to from here, we ask ourselves?
The streets of Durban have been swept clean;
The rubble of Pietermaritzburg has been carted away;
Many small towns and villages have created some order;
And the N3 has been re-opened and the supply chain
    restored.

And still a question hangs ever over our heads:
WHERE TO FROM HERE?
Words and slogans have flashed across our media:
Structural change, Political re-shuffling, a more shared
    economy –
And again: All of the above and so much more.

Yes – I echo that!
And still my question does not leave me:
Where to from here? How do I help to fix this?
Me: A daughter. A mother. A woman of faith?
And there is but one answer I hear through all the
    overwhelming voices:
One stitch at a time, with that which lies deep within:
The joint threads of our humanity!

Jointly –
With our tiered hands and shattered hearts;
With our anger and anguish;
With our despair and desperation;
With our fear and fatigue;
With our patience and kindness;
With our kindness and encouragement;
With our humanity and our humility;
With hope and help from he who has gone before us:
Our gracious Lord, Jesus Christ.
With faith and grace!
We will help stitch this back together!
One community at a time.
One person at a time.
One human being to another at a time.
One stitch at a time!

People are living here

Yesterday
I sat in a car and watched life unfold.
Life of rural Kwazulu-Natal;
Life as I saw it through the naked eye.
On the dusty roads of villages
I saw people who live and create life
In this vast expanse
Of rolling hills and green veld, interspersed by thorn trees;
Of grazing cows, bleating goats and chickens crossing the
    road.
And a voice echoed into my heart:
People are living here!

People are living here –
So vastly differently from my own life.
It is the sunrise and sunset that dictates the rhythm of their
    day;
It is the seasons of the year that give life structure.
It is weather conditions that dictate the agenda of a 24-hour
    cycle.
It is natures rhythm that dictates the
Everyday chores
Of fetching water, washing clothes and planting crops.
And for a moment it seems
So much simpler than what I know
Of my own life, dictated by my alarm clock, the internet
And appointments jotted down in my diary.

People are living here – I think to myself,
As I watch women return from washing their clothes
In the river that flows in the valley.
It is these women who open my eyes to this:
Community is lived here,
And I rest for a moment in their space,
In the beauty around me,
In the simplicity of their rhythm.

And yet I know that
At a glance and for a moment
Life seems simpler, slower, easier
And I treasure the moment I can rest in it;
But I know that
Beyond the beauty of the veld and the thorn trees
Is a reality much more jarring than the naked eye can see,
A reality that is built on the other side
Of the deep-running crack
That divides our country and our world.

It runs on the other side of the deep crevice the separates
The haves and the have nots,
The employed and the unemployed,
Those who have running water and those who don't;
The ones who have a multitude of choices they can make
    daily
And those whose choices are so limited
Because of the side of the crack they were born on.

And I cannot but ask myself:
Is there anything that unites us
That can ease the pain in my soul
Over the reality of this ever-growing crack in the world?
Is there anything that does not divide us?
Something bigger than ourselves
That unites instead of tearing us apart?
I breathe a little lighter as I find the answer in a little
    church:
Nestled between the branches of big green trees
A rusted roof, a few broken windows and a battered door.
It is here that I find that speck of hope my soul longs for,
That little bit in the world that bridges the gap.
A church that stands: a symbol of faith.
This speck of the knowledge that we are all united
By the breath God gave us
At the beginning of life.
Life-giving breath.
And with the breath we are given from our Creator comes
Hope for a lighter tomorrow,
Faith in the power of love shared in community,
Grace for the broken pieces of life,
And our God-given dignity for all.
Created in His image,
Which no crack in the world can separate.
A dignity that is not ours to own,
Dignity whose worth is not ours to decide.
God-given, life-giving dignity for all people.
No matter where
People are living!

African child – this is for you

African child – this is for you:
As I watch you it warms my heart.
You sing and move with such rhythm,
My feet cannot but tap to the heartbeat of your song.
I watch you playing with such natural joy.
A soccer ball made of discarded plastic packets;
A punctured tyre being rolled down the road.
You run along the streets of your village with
No shoes and dust covering your young feet.
The sun of Africa comes up as a smile washes over your face.
African child – you teach me much:
The joy in the simple things in life.
You sit in a classroom and your voice rings deep inside of me
As you recite the alphabet with conviction and pride.
African child this is for you.

BUT
I have no right to romanticise your life
As there is little romance in it.
You were born into a broken world;
You were born into the deep-running cracks.
You had no choice in this.
For now, your innocence protects you from the reality of
    what this means;
For now, you hold the space, not understanding the reality
    of this truth;
For now, you find the simple things in the cracks that give
    you an innocent joy.

But as your feet grow and you search for bigger shoes to fit
You will realise the world is not fair.
It is broken!
And you will begin to realise what it means
That you were born into the cracks;
The choices that lie ahead for you will probably be much
    harder to make.
The vulnerability that comes with living in the cracks will
    become evident
As the innocent rhythm of your soul takes you into
    adulthood that you will need to master.

African child,
I have no right to romanticise your vibrant dance, your
    sunny smile, nor your simple play:
There is no romance in it.
And yet – today –
I thank you for it.
Because it is this, Your innocent childhood,
That warms my heart and sings a deep melody in my soul.
It opens my eyes to the value of the simple things in life.
So, today I thank you for this,
African Child.

THE WORD
BECAME FLESH

Reflections from scripture ....

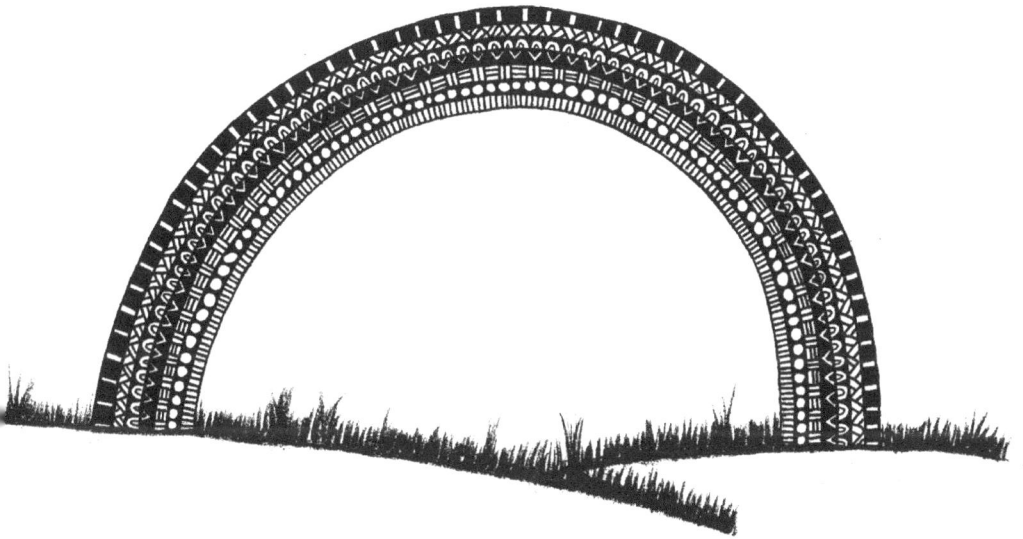

Powerful

The Word became flesh and dwelt amongst us

The Word –
God Himself
God – Creator of the universe –
Who spoke, and there was!
There was light
There was land
There was day and there was night.
Your words have POWER
To create
To order
To direct
To command
And there is
And there was

YET –
You left this place of power
You left the realms of heaven
You departed from your place of command
You gave it up
To be helpless
To be feeble
To be powerless

In human form You came
In a stable – a barn – a shack
On the outskirts of Bethlehem
In this nondescript place
You became someone
With no power.
As you lay there in a manger – a helpless baby
At the mercy of your parents –
You
A mighty, powerful God
Entered a world struggling for power
Powerless.

This
I struggle to understand
Why?
Why give it up?
For what?
Then I see the shepherds –
Rugged, scruffy, men
Who rushed to see You.
They were powerless people too
It was them
The angels sent to find You,
The powerful God in a powerless state.
It was they who saw You and recognised
Who You are.
They saw in this powerless baby
The powerful God they so longed to meet.
They were the ones who were the first
And they were the ones who recognised

Your power
In Your powerlessness

They recognised You
The One Who comes to be with us,
To be in solidarity with humanity.
To walk with us through the shredded pieces of our lives.
To not only stand with us,
Or be with us,
But to be
Us.
To be
Human.

And as You did this
You revealed to us Your light
A light that the darkness could not overcome.

Your power is not powerless –
In fact, it is not feeble and helpless –
BUT a power that stands
Midst the shattered lives we live
Midst the darkness of this world
Because Yours is a power that is greater,
That stands and brings hope, joy and peace
Even when our world falls apart.

Yours is the power that brings
Healing, restoration, reconciliation and renewal.
It brings something greater than war, revenge and control
    can.

Yours is
The power of love.
Love that does not want to dictate,
But love that wants to enrich.

As I watch you –
Helpless, powerless baby
Lying in a manger –
I allow Your story to unfold in front of me.
And I grasp something about Your powerless state:
It is a power that remains steadfast
Even when around us the powers that be seem to be in
     control.

It is power and has power
To change
To restore
To bring peace
A peace we all so long for
With each other
And with ourselves.

It is a power that gently holds
The crushed heart and slowly brings it back to life.
It is a power that turns fists of rage and revenge
Into hands that can reach out and be reconciled.
It is a power that reaches into our souls with truth
And gives us the ability to acknowledge our shortcomings
Without being drowned by shame.

A power that makes us
More humble
More gentle
More kind
More.

It is a power that speaks new life
Into the battered, self-inflicted self-doubt
And restores our sense of worth.

It is a power that continues to shine
A light that never goes out,
A light that the darkness does not overcome.

Powerful God,
You were – You are – You will be.
You spoke and there was.
Baby lying in a manger –

Powerless God
Yet God of power –
We invite You in,
Into the powerless places of our lives,
Into the scared world we live in
Be light in us
Be love in us
Be peace in us
Powerless child
This Christmas we pray
Be powerful within us.

Mary

Mary: Tonight, I wonder what went through you heart
What captivated your thoughts
As you watched your baby asleep on the hay.
I imagine there was a deep joy, the
Joy of a mother holding a new life.
A joy deep within;
A joy words fail to express.
I imagine a deep peace that held your soul
As you held your baby boy – Immanuel –
God with us.
I imagine hope.
A hope for this child and the life that lies ahead.
Hope for His future filled with colour and laughter.
Hope.
Mary, as I wonder
I imagine it was this that held you that night:
Joy, Peace and Hope.

Mary, I assume you did not imagine that night
What this joy, peace and hope would in reality turn into.
How joy would be ripped from your soul one day.
How your heart would be shattered
And the peace you felt that night would be broken to pieces
As darkness fell over the land.
How hope would drain out of you
As you listened to crowds call out crucify, crucify!
Mary, I imagine you did not expect that that perfect night
Would end in this way.

And yet, Mary, you would later understand
The things you treasured and pondered in your heart.
You would understand that these things –
Joy, Peace and Hope that knit you together that night in the
    stable,
That glued you together as mother and child –
Were exactly the things that your baby boy, Jesus,
Would bring into the world.

They would expand beyond the horizon of your lives
Into such far reaching places that you didn't even know
    existed.
They would permeate the lives of those whom your Son
    would meet
On the dusty roads of Galilee.
And they would change the course of history
To the ends of the earth.

Mary, you would later grasp this:
Joy, Peace and Hope were never meant for you and Him
    alone –
They were meant for all people!
They would change and restore the world.
Your Son, Jesus, would take them along
As He walked the roads and changed lives.
He would heal the sick, restore the broken hearted.
He would feed the masses, and still the storm.
He would reach out to the marginalised and lonely and
He would speak with authority and challenge power.
He would show the world – by stepping into it –
How Peace, Joy and Hope could be found

In Him, for all people,
The Word made flesh.

Mary
I wish those last days with your baby boy could have looked
    different.
I wish you didn't have to lose Joy, Peace and Hope
At the foot of that cross.
No mother should have to experience the darkness of that
    hour.
Watching your child suffer such innocent pain
Hearing Him speak: It is finished.
No mother should have to watch her child
Bow his head and give up his spirit.
I imagine it was so dark within your soul in that moment
    that
You couldn't even wonder where God – Immanuel – had
    gone.

But, Mary, we know this story did not end in darkness,
We know this story carries on.
When, early in the morning "on the first day of the week",
While you sat in the darkness of your grief,
Maybe remembering this night of joy in Bethlehem.
It was your fellow sisters who found the stone rolled away
And they returned, calling this message into your foggy
    mind:
The Lord has risen!
And through the darkness of your soul a light began to
    shine through and
Joy, peace and hope sapped back into your body

Like a new breath of life.
Could it be?
Jesus – the One Who saves.

And you remembered the things you pondered in your
    heart
On that first night in Bethlehem, as you watched your baby
    sleep.
Slowly the pieces of the puzzle fell into place before your
    eyes
And you saw the bigger picture:
You saw the depth of JOY, PEACE and HOPE.
Joy to the world, the Lord has come
And peace on earth and goodwill to all people
And hope to the nations.
Joy, peace, hope for you, for me, for all.
And you experience the message unfold in your heart.
You finally understand what it was really about:
For God so loved the world!

For God so loved the world ....

For God so loved the world
It is impossible for me to understand
A love that stands so strong and bold
A love that is steadfast and never grows cold.
A love that says YES to each as we are
A love that never stops, whether near or far
A love that stands firm in the sorrow of life
A love that affirms whatever the fight.
A love so passionate and kind
A love that sees; it is not blind

It sees the world and its broken mess
It sees the heart and much distress
It sees the sadness in the grieving eyes
It see the face that never lies
It sees the disappointment of shattered dreams
It sees the fists curled up for revenge
It sees the heart smeared with smudges of guilt
It sees the soul that is defenceless and scared
It sees straight into the places we try to hide
It sees every time we were silent and cried

It is a love, so strong and wise
It is a love we cannot begin to surmise
It is a love that wants the world to know:
I am here, I will heal you, I will put on a show
A show that begins in a small kind of place
A show that is not clean and yet full of Grace

A show that only few were aware
Began in a stable somewhere out there

It began with angels that appeared full of light
It began with shepherds' hearts full of fright.
It began when they rushed to go and see
It began when Jesus was born to set the world free
He was born to live and show and reign
In a world so shattered on so much terrain
To show the world The Love of God
To show our hearts that God is good
To show the way of joy and cheer
To show the way out of darkness and fear
To show us the way God would want us to walk
To show us a way of a new kind of talk

A talk that is wholesome and gives us strength
A talk that makes it possible that all have a friend
A talk that is made up of words that build up
A talk that considers everyone's broken heart

He came to show the heart of God
For us to follow in His footsteps and never give up
He was born for us to lighten the load
He was born and encourages us to be strong and bold
He was born to live not only then
He was born to live in our hearts even when
Life is hard and the road is tough
He was born for us to know He is enough

Enough to fill all spaces with love
A love that began in the heavens above
A love designed by our Creator before all time
A love that says, I give you what is Mine
My Son will come and dwell on earth
And lead you to a place of peace

A handful of ashes

A handful of Ashes is
All that is left behind
In the wake of fires
Of missiles and bombs
All that is left behind
Of revenge and hate
All that is left behind
Of a fiery tongue that spat out
Raging, destructive words.

A handful of ashes.

Ashes
Scattered between,
A pile of rubble
Of pain
Of destruction
Of fear
Silently telling a story
Of an angry war that blazed through this place.

Ashes
Wordless
Nothing.

And then I see
You
Quietly walking among the wreckage
You bend down,
You scoop up
A handful of ashes.
And
You begin to walk
To meet those who have quietly gathered around.
The child. The orphan.
The homeless. The widow.
The father. The mother.
The friend. The enemy.
The rich man. The beggar.
The people.
The faces.

At each of them You stop
Looking gently into their eyes
Eyes that speak
Of pain and distress
Of anger and disappointment
Of hopelessness and despair
Of fear and grief
Of guilt and shame
Of that which is broken …
You see much more than human eyes
You see the untold stories written across their faces

Silently
You dip Your finger into
The handful of ashes
And gently draw a cross
On each forehead
Just above the eyes
Where the wordless story lives

Then You find me
And you do the same
You look deep into my eyes
You see my own muted story
And you mark my forehead too
With a cross
Your cross
From a handful of ashes.

I will give up and give ...
(Mark 14:3-9)

I ask myself what is it that I will "give up for Lent" this year?
My eyes take an inventory of all the things I could –
Food, drink, activities… many things appear before my eyes.
What should I give up?
The question echoes in my mind.

And then I discover you and your story –
Woman without a name.
You came with an alabaster jar of very expensive perfume:
PURE NARD.
You broke this jar and
You poured the nard
On Jesus's head.
I don't know what it cost but
I assume you gave up a lot
In order to give.

You gave
From a heart that recognised Who Jesus was.
From your heart
You poured without holding back.
You broke and emptied without hesitation
And the fragrance of this act
Filled the room.
You gave.

You gave up
In order to give.
So, this Lent
I too want to give up
In order to give.
Give without holding back,
Pour without hesitation.
Break the jar and let the fragrance of Christ
Fill the space around.

I will give up Despair
And GIVE Hope!
I will give up Resentfulness
And GIVE Forgiveness
I will give up Doubt
And GIVE Trust.
I will give up Hate
And GIVE Peace.
I will give up Pride
And GIVE Humility.

I will give up me
And I will give You.
I will break the jar and
I will pour You into the world
Without holding back:
You, Jesus Christ
God of Hope
God of Grace
God of Peace
God of Love.

This Lent –
I will give up ME
And give
YOU!

In His footsteps ...
(John 13:1-17)

I sat in the shadows
Watching Him
Whose path I had chosen to follow.
In His footsteps I have walked.

I sat and watched Him
As He wrapped a towel around His waist and began
He kneeled at each of His disciples' feet
One by one
Gently taking their feet into His hands
And pouring water over them,
Washing them, cleaning them
Of the dust of the day's walk.
There was silence;
Complete stillness around the table.
No one spoke
No one moved.

I looked down at my own feet:
Dusty, grubby, filthy,
Not only from the walk of the day
But from the walk of life.
I remembered where these feet have walked:
Walked away from those I was called to care for;
Walked away from those in desperate need of compassion;
Walked away from those I couldn't forgive.
Dusty, grubby, filthy feet,

How often have they walked away!

I remembered how they have walked into places
Places I call: I want – Me
They have carried me into places of greed and longing for
    wealth
They have carried me into pride and arrogance
They have carried me into disregard of another and their
    God given dignity
Dusty, grubby, filthy feet.
How often have they not walked into places
Where it was all about me.

I remembered how they have walked though rough terrain.
They have walked through many moments of
    disappointment and injury.
They have walked through many times of grief and pain.
They have walked through many spaces of suffering and
    despair.
Dusty, grubby, filthy feet,
How often have they not stumbled along the rough terrain
    of life
That hurt my soul.

My feet – these feet – have
Walked many roads in life.
My thoughts still drifted far away,
Along the roads my feet have walked,
When I felt His shadow fall across me.
There He was: standing before me.
Then He kneeled down

And He took my feet
One at a time,
Letting the cool water wash over them.
Letting the water do what it does:
Rinsing – cleaning – removing
That which clung to my soles.
Refreshing.
Renewing.
Water from His hands –
Life-giving water –
Flowing over my dusty, grubby, filthy feet.

Then He took the towel
And he dried my weary feet
And gently put them back on the ground.
And something was different.
They felt new,
They felt restored,
They felt fresh:
They felt they could walk again,
Walk along the road that followed Him.
They could walk again –
In His footsteps.

Barabbas – What did you do with your freedom?
(Luke 23:18-24)

Barabbas –
I walked along a lake last evening
In the stillness of the evening
I let my mind wander
I let my imagination follow the story line
Of what happened there
In Jerusalem
On the fateful Friday

My mind conjured up images of
A crowd
Noisy
Shouting
Demanding
Choosing
You – Barabbas –
To be released
Freed from death-row
Free to go!

A man stood elevated addressing this crowd
"Who do you want me to set free?"
Leaving the choice over to them –
To the people –
Allowing their voice to be the jury
Over
Jesus or you.

The choice was theirs!

Barabbas
The people chose you!
They shouted so loudly
That Pilate let you go.
You, Barabbas!
You, who had blood on your hands
While another
Jesus
Innocent
Ended on the cross
Where His hands
Dripped with blood
From the solid nails that held Him there.

Barabbas,
I wonder,
What did you do
When you left the chains of prison behind?
Did you go with the crowd to the cross?
Did you celebrate your freedom with your friends?
Did you plan the next act of violence?
Did the anger still drive you to lash out, to destroy,
To kill?

Or,
Barabbas,
Did you stop to let it all sink in?
Did you stop for a moment and reflect?
An innocent man's hands dripping with blood

For the blood on yours!
Did you take in the magnitude of what had just happened?
An innocent man's life
In exchange for
Your guilt-ridden one.

Did it soften your heart?
Did it change something inside you?

Barabbas,
What did you do?
You went free
While He hung on the cross
Where you should have hung.

Barabbas,
I wonder:
What happened to you?
Most of all I wonder:
What did you do with your freedom?

I stop along the lake
I look out over the water
Still deep in thought.
Barabbas,
What did you do with your freedom.?

Deep in thought
My eyes meet the water –
And I see the outline of my own reflection
Looking back at me
The question echoing inside my soul

What did you do with your freedom?

Who will roll the stone away?
(Mark 16:3-4)

I wake early,
The sun not yet up,
And my thoughts take me to the women –
Subdued, grief-stricken, paralysed, traumatised
Women –
Walking to the grave
On that first day of the week.
They walk, their steps slow and tired,
Their minds in a fog because of what just happened in their
    lives
Not able to grasp it all –
Not yet, anyway.
For now
They are walking as if in some bad dream.
Only a practicality works itself to the surface of their minds:

"Who will roll the stone away?"

It is still dark – the sun has not risen.
I lie there in the safety of my bed
Reflecting on this scene
And this question:
Who will roll the stone away?
For me, it's not a practicality.

For me, this question is one about life:
My life.
I recognise the stones
The rocks
The boulders
Blocking me from living

Boulders of
Pride
Fear
Grief
Guilt
Shame
Insecurities
Big, solid, heavy rocks
At the entrance
Which is also the exit
Of my own heart and my own soul.

Who will roll that stone away?
Who will help me move those rocks
So I that can live!
So that I can breathe
So that I can have joy
So that I can experience hope
So that my heart can be full?

Who will roll the stone away?
So that fresh air can move
Through these suffocating spaces inside,
So that light can shine

In the darkness of my inner world.
So that I can release
That which holds me captive,
So that I can give and receive love
Without fear of rejection and judgement.

Who will roll the stone away?

As the dawn breaks,
As the light starts making itself
Tenderly into the darkness of the night
My thoughts arrive
At the empty tomb.

Who will roll the stone away?
And there, before me, lies the answer:

"I HAVE!"

FROM A MOTHER'S HEART

I held a new born today ....

I held a new-born today
I felt her new life against my own body
I saw her perfect little fingers curled up in little fists
I felt her steady breath against my cheek
I saw her sleep peacefully in my presence

In this moment I realised
Contrary to everything around me
Contrary to all the hardship I see
Contrary to all the pain and suffering any given day throws
    at us
Contrary to all the wars fought and battles raging
Contrary to all the vengeful words uttered and hate felt
Contrary to all the sadness expressed and despair uttered
Contrary to all of this – and so much more –
I believe in the good

I believe that good is still
The greater power in this world of ours
I believe that in this world
Good still lives and reigns and has it's being
Midst the world that tries to convince me otherwise
Midst those who shake their heads at my optimism
I believe in the good

I believe in the power of love
I believe in the power of kindness and hope
I believe in the power of mercy and grace
I believe in the power of forgiveness and peace
I believe in the power of generosity and care
Contrary to so much darkness in the world
I believe in light.

I held a new-born today
I believe this for her
For her new perfect little life
I believe this for next generations
Because
The One who made her
The One who formed her in her innermost being
The One who set this life and universe into motion
The One who directs the stars on their courses
The One who is: Yesterday – Today – Tomorrow
Is GOOD

I held a new-born today
Contrary to so much
I believe in the good
For me
For us
For her

A Mother's Plea ...

Please STOP
Stop the bombs
Stop the killing
Stop the destruction

Please stop
So that our children can go out again:
Into the sunlight and not the dust
Into green places and not rubble
So that they can go out
And be safe under the blue sky
That stretches across borders
That we have made
To divide us from them

Please STOP
So that our children can breathe in fresh air
So that they can know and grasp that
They have a right
To feel
To be
Safe

Please STOP
So that our children learn that
There is a greater power in the world
A greater power
Than hate and revenge

Please stop
So that we the adults can teach them
To love our neighbour
To honour the sanctity of life
To respect another
Even when that person is different
In colour, creed, culture

Please stop
So that our children do not make hate
Their norm
But so that
They can believe
In the good
In peace

Please stop
So that they can experience these things
Goodness – Safety – Peace
So that this becomes
Their normal
And will in years to come
Teach this norm
To their children

PLEASE STOP!

Because I am your mother ...

I remember that day –
The first day we were separated from each other.
It had been a long day of waiting:
Waiting for you to take your own first breath;
Waiting for you to open your eyes;
Waiting for you to leave my body and be your very own
    person
Separate from me.
It was a miracle day
When I finally held you in my arms
And your eyes opened and you were there.
A miracle of new life – your life –
Lying in my arms.

I will never forget that day
And that moment when life, my life, changed for ever.
You changed me.
You changed me into someone who now –
Somehow –
Lives two lives.
Yours and mine.
My heart no longer beats only within my chest
But it now beats somewhere
Out there too,
Wherever you are.

I remember how
My heart swelled with pride with every milestone you
    achieved.
My heart sang with joy when you spoke your first word –
When you took your first step – when you ate your
    vegetables –
Holding your own spoon.
Every step of the way
I watched in awe as you ventured out into life,
As you grew in curiosity and discovered the world.
My heart beat twice every time.
And my heart was there,
Protecting and nurturing and encouraging you
Every step of the way.

As you have grown older
This feeling of wanting to protect you has grown
Because I long to protect you
From what lies ahead.
I wish I could protect you from
Heartache and disappointment,

In others and in yourself.
I wish you did not have to face the failure and setbacks
That make your heart tumble into despair.
I wish I could protect you from the conflict and rejection
That shatters your sense of worth.
I wish I could make those difficult choices
That will tear you apart.
I wish I could spare you the reality of being disappointed
And disillusioned

In others and in life.
Oh, how I have wished to protect you from it all.

But this is not life, my child.
It never was and never will be
And to protect you is not my job;
Not anymore.
Not as you have grown older and are becoming
A man.
I have wrestled with this
As you have stepped into this space we call
Adulthood.
I have lain awake at night and worried
Whether you will cope with what lies ahead.
I have cried tears as I have seen you struggle with life's
        challenges.
I have been angry when you made your own choices
That made me scared.

My son,
I wish I could protect you – but I can't.
The road that lies ahead is yours to walk.
It is your journey and not mine.
And I hope that you will walk that road with confidence,
That you will have taken from your childhood some things
I tried to instil into your heart and your soul.

I hope you will be kind
To others and yourself.
I hope that after rejection you will draw together the
        frazzled threads

Of your self-esteem and learn to embrace your worth
Again.
I hope that after every fall you will dig deep
And find the courage to rise and carry on
And, if you need to, start again.
I hope you will honour people always
And see in each person a unique creation of God.
I hope you find friends who will encourage you and cheer
    you on
To be the best version of yourself,
And that you will be that friend to others.
I hope you will never let fear of the unknown stop you
But that you will be brave and step out anyway.
I hope that you will make good choices
And that, when you choose badly, you will never forget that
You can choose again.
I hope you will find moments of complete peace
That reassure you: You are not alone.
Your Maker is always near.
I hope you remain curious about life,
With all its facets and colours,
And that your life grows rich and meaningful.

This is my hope,
My wish,
As you step into this space called
Adulthood.
It's not always easy;
Sometimes it becomes very hard.
But remember:
You are never alone

As my heart still beats for every beat of yours.
I will be here, always:
Cheering you on;
Helping you up;
Wiping the tears away;
Celebrating your successes;
And loving you through your failures.
I will be here
Always.
Because
I am
Your mother.

FAITH – HOPE – LOVE

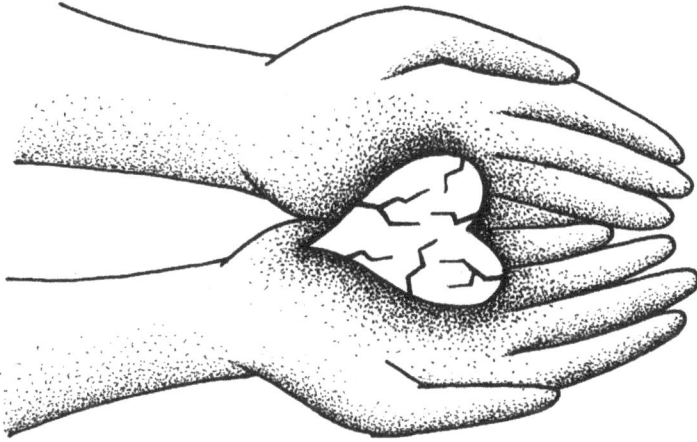

Woman – I heard about your faith

You – woman –
Caught in the crossfire of a senseless war,
Finding yourself standing helplessly
While bombs and miles threaten your lives
You stand protecting your children in your arms
Praying for safety
Praying for an end to the madness
Praying for peace in your land
Praying to the One Who you know is
Complete love
Complete peace
Your prayers deeply rooted in the goodness of God
Woman – I heard about your faith

You – woman –
Making your way across a desolate land
Desperate to find a place for your children
Where they can play safely in the streets
Where they can go to school and learn
Where they can grow up knowing
There are places in the world where they are safe
Woman – I heard about your journey
That turned your identity from a citizen into a refugee
Because you had hope for something better
Because you believed that God had a place for you
Your hope deeply rooted in your Lord
Who has a hope and a future for you!
Woman – I heard about your faith

You – woman –
Building a life from rubble
Rising from the ashes of destruction
To rebuild with courage
With inner strength and patience
For yourself – for generations to come
You're building life
With nothing but a handful of nothing
But a soul of hope
And a heart that believes there is something
Waiting beyond the horizon of your now
Your trust deeply rooted in the One
Who has gone ahead of you to prepare a place
Woman – I heard about your faith

You – woman –
Alone and frightened
On a road away,
Away from the abuse and destructive words of another
To find a place
Where you are valued
Where you are treasured
Where your self-worth is celebrated
And your dignity is upheld and not smashed to pieces
By a fit of rage and violence

I see how your eyes were opened to the beauty of who you
    are
And the dignity that was instilled in you by your Creator
It was like a veil being lifted from your eyes
When you realised: This was not love and

You deserved more
And deep in your heart there was a new heartbeat of worth
Instilled by He who made all things good
And with this faith you walked forward
Your mind deeply rooted anew in the knowledge:
I am wonderfully and beautifully made
Woman – I heard about your faith

You – woman –
Finding yourself in the midst of the consequences
Consequences of bad choices and destructive behaviour
I see how you have taken it
How you have owned it
How you have dug deep to expose the guilt and the shame
How you have risen
And humbly asked of the other
Forgive me, for I have sinned.
Forgive me
Your heart dug deep to reach that place of
"My grace is sufficient for you"
Woman – I heard about your faith

You – woman –
With a crushed heart because of a wrong
Someone inflicted on you
I see the fight in your spirit
The fight against resentfulness and revenge
You battle out inside
And then you reach out
You forgive
You restore that which was broken

With a gentle heart and a quiet gesture
It is forgiven, you say
Woman – I heard about your generous heart
Rooted deeply in this:
Forgive as the Lord forgave
Woman – I heard about your faith

You – woman –
Joining hands with others
Side by side to bring about wholeness and goodness
In community
Building, sharing, giving
Love and joy and peace
Woman – I heard about your community
I heard about how you united to serve
To serve one another
To serve your community
To give that which heals.
This rooted, deeply rooted, in the calling of Christ
Serve as I have served
Woman – I heard about your faith

Women of Faith
It is this that unites you
To me – to us – to each other
Across oceans and continents
Across language and cultural barriers
Across creed and ethnicity
United through this invisible bond
Called faith that we share
Let us continue to hear our stories of faith

And be encouraged and strengthened in our walk
Not by sight, but by faith

Women across the world
We heard about your faith

You drew a line in the sand!

You drew a line in the sand –
Maybe the most courageous line you ever drew in your life.
A line that marked the end.
A line that marked a new beginning!
You drew a line in the sand!

With courage, determination and an inner strength
You stepped over that line.
That line marks your decision to leave the old and believe in
    the new.
The line marks the end of accepting:
Destructive words that shamed and blamed you;
Destructive words that eroded your self-worth and your
    beautiful soul;
Destructive words that ate away your courage, your energy
    and your zest for life;
Destructive words that slowly but surely depleted you of
    compassion and kindness;
Destructive words that left you a shell of who you are!
YOU drew a line in the sand.

You stepped over that line!
Now, as you continue to walk on the other side of this line
Dig deep and keep walking
Dig deep and keep searching and hoping
Dig deep and keep trusting in the new, that will blossom.
Dig deep, knowing
That midst the ashes of your empty soul

YOU are still there.
The seeds of your beautiful being
Lie scattered on the dusty floor of your empty shell
But they are still there.

Water those seeds
Water those seeds with compassion and kindness;
Water those seeds with patience and self-care;
Water those seeds daily.
Water them with the tears of grief for what was on the other
    side of the line.
Water them and nurture them
And trust that from the ashes will grow a new life.

Hold on tightly to HOPE.
Hope that your creative being will come alive again;
Hope that your trust in the good of others can be restored;
Hope that your zest for life can return!

You drew a line in the sand.
That doesn't mean the journey of healing is over.
It doesn't mean that the pain on the other side of the line
    won't come crashing over you;
It doesn't mean that the shame you feel has stopped
    running deep in your veins;
It doesn't mean you no longer carry the heavy questions of
    "should I" or "could I";
It doesn't mean the voices of blame have simply gone silent;
It doesn't mean the guilt piled on you has evaporated into
    thin air;
It doesn't mean the road ahead is a walk in the park.

BUT it DOES mean THIS:
With courage, determination and inner strength,
You stepped over into the new;
BECAUSE
You drew a line in the sand.

Safe places

I always thought it was love –
An unconditional kind of love – that
My heart searched for
My heart ached for
My heart needed.
But I discovered that
This really was not it.
It was actually always
Something else.
It was –
It is –
To feel safe.

Safety.
Not for my successes
Not for my confidence and drive
Not for my humour and creativity
The safety in these things
I found easily in my life.

But a safety from something else
A safety for the internal battles I fight.
A safe place
Where I know
I will not be abandoned, rejected and judged
Because I am afraid and vulnerable and broken;
Because I don't have all the answers;
Because I don't know where to go with the next step;

Because I messed up and made bad choices;
Because I don't have it all worked out;
Because I don't know how to take the next step;
Because I am afraid;
Because I am afraid to say I am afraid;
Because I am scared of not being safe;
Because I am insecure and fragile.

I have been searching for a safe place,
Where my story does not have to be clean;
Nor does it all need to be written on straight lines;
Nor do all the sentences have to be finished and complete.
Where I can contradict myself because I don't know
Or because it's both and
Not one or the other.
Where I am not finished – not at all –
But always a work in progress.

Where I can sob and have a messy face;
Where my make-up is smudged and my face is pale
And my hair a mess.
Where I am confused about myself.
Where I don't know what I want,
Never mind what I need.
Where my feelings seem to contradict each other
And my thoughts are still not clear.

I was searching for this:
A place
Where all of this
And so much more
Was safe!
Safe from rejection, judgement and abandonment,
The things I fear most in life.

Because I realised
That when I find this safe place
There I will find
Love.

A God Love
In a messy, broken, hard world.
A place
Where I no longer need to be afraid
But I am safe.

And God said: It is not good that you are alone .... and God made friends

The beauty of friendship
The need for friendship
The gift of friendship
We should celebrate this more.

It is not good to be alone.
A fundamental human need is to belong,
And friendship is this beautiful place that fills this need:
Belonging, affirming, safety.
To have a place to live,
To breathe, to be human.
To be.

I have many friends – and oh, they all have a special place
In the kaleidoscope of my life.

There are the patient listeners.
Those who listen till the last bit of detail of my story
Has tumbled from my lips,
Not interrupting, not taking away from the colourful
    experience,
Just listening.
And then they smile,
Affirming that they heard me
And were joyful to hear the colourful tale.

There are the patient waiters.
Those who wait, and wait and wait some more,
For as long as it takes,
Holding the space until that last sob has been gasped from
    my soul.
The tear-catchers and hope-holders,
Never doubting that the flood of tears will end
And I will be able to breathe more lightly again.
When the wave of grief has finally crashed
And ebbed out onto the beach of life.

There are the trust givers.
Those who place into my hands the thing we call trust.
They lay out in my presence the bruised places of their
    hearts
And the scarred shreds of their souls
And the fears that run deep in their bellies.
They do a brave thing –
They expose themselves and give to me
A piece of their humanity and vulnerability
And whisper:
I trust you with me.

There are the anxious thought carriers.
The ones that have patience to wait,
Wait till my mind has calmed and the fog has lifted
And then speak calm and peace back
Into a mind that could not stop for hours on end.
While on a roller coaster of thoughts,
They are the ones who then help me separate

Truth from misplaced imagination.
And see: It is good.

There are the voices of reason.
The ones who stop me from whatever high I am on
Or whatever depth of despair I am in.
The voice that speaks through the jumble of emotion
The voice of reason.
A voice God made (sometimes) I think,
Especially for me.

There are the cheerleaders and hand clappers,
For every achievement, on whatever level.
The ones who shout, or whisper, or simply speak:
You have done this!
You can do it!
Don't stop now!

There are the fear holders who,
When it is scary to take the next step,
When the thought of potential failure
Or rejection, criticism or failure,
Makes me feel glued to the ground.
They are the ones who say:
Let me hold your fear for a while
While you take the next step.

There are the truth speakers.
The ones who will speak the truth.
They will sometimes wait until the time is right

And the truth can be heard,
Absorbed, grow and flourish,
Into something beautiful and new.
But the truth they will speak.

There are the peace makers.
Those who sit at the negotiation table so long
While I fire endless missiles of self-doubt,
Insecurities and self-hate at my already battered soul.
They are the ones who sit for as long as it takes
Until there is peace inside:
Peace with myself,
Peace with who I am.

And then there are:
The faith holders and prayer warriors,
The silent voices and invisible faces,
Who continue to believe,
Who continue to pray,
Who never stop believing
Quietly, consistently, loyally
In me
And for me.

And God said: It is not good that she is alone.
Alone with
The nooks and crannies of her life,
With her heart and her soul,
With the things that are visible to herself and the world
And the blind spots and the messiness of her life.

It is not good that she is alone
With her beauty and vulnerability,
With her strength her of fears,
With her humanity.

And God made my friends.
Thank You, Lord!

Helpless Hands

I look back on it.
I remember seeing you look at me,
Seeing me and my distress laid bare in front of you.
You saw the anxiety that ran deep in my veins;
You saw the sense of hopelessness beating in my heart;
You saw my eyes search for a future that I simply could not
    see.

Then I remember how you looked at your hands.
It seemed to me you felt so helpless,
That your hands felt so empty.
I sensed you so wanted to do something
With your hands
To get me to the other side.
But how could you do this
With (what seemed like) your own helpless hands?

I look back at it
And I can tell you that, even if your hands seemed
Empty, helpless, weak to you,
They were not!
It was those hand that filled mine to overflowing.
It was those hands that made mine gain strength.

It was your hands that went inside your heart
Where they found a huge supply of compassion
And quietly you took some of that
And just passed it on to me.

It was those hands that unpacked your own story
And gently handed it to me,
So that I knew in no uncertain terms that
I was not alone with my story.
It was another's story too – and you survived.

It was those hands that grabbed some of your own hope
And poured this hope into my hands,
And your hands directed me to a place
Where I could breathe a little lighter as I knew
This was just a part of the journey
And not the end of the road.

It was those hands that reached out
And held my body as it shook with fear
So that I did not crumble into despair
But recognised that I was held by the strength
Of your hands.

It was your hands that you folded in prayer.
You took what felt so heavy in my heart
And placed it into God's hands
So that my soul could rest in the hands of your prayers
When my hands were unable to fold into each other.

It was your hands that blessed me
And reassured me that we have a God
"Who will never leave or forsake us"
And it gave me courage to place my trembling hands
Back into His
And it kindled my faith back into this reassurance:

You hold me by my right hand.

I want to reassure you today that
Those hands, your hands, were never helpless hands.
They were hopeful hands.
They were caring hands.
They were strong hands.
They were faithful hands.
They were sharing hands.
They were healing hands.

Most of all
They were helpful hands.
They placed what you had
Into my empty and helpless ones.
So that mine are now
Full,
Hopeful,
Stronger
Hands.

Buried pain

I didn't know you were still there.
I didn't realise how you lay dormant for so long,
Deeply hidden away somewhere in my heart.
Life had seemed colourful;
Life had been an adventure;
Life had been okay –
Or so I thought.
And yet you were there.
Somewhere behind high walls,
Tucked away,
Quietly occupying a space within.

And then
Something touched your space.
Something shook your walls,
Something broke you open.
I'm not really sure what it was.
A word someone spoke?
An action that unsettled?
Or was it a smell or a sound?
Something shook the foundation of your walls
And you broke open.
I could not stop what happened.
I could not stop the anger that tumbled out.
I could not stop the tears that flooded my eyes.
I could not stop the despair that drained
Through the cracks.
I could not stop the wall from tumbling down

And exposing you:
Buried pain.

What I did not know –
But what you knew well –
Is that you waited a long time to be released,
To be freed from this place inside.
Now I am grateful that
You found a way out.
You found a way through the cracks.
You found a way to break the walls down.
You found a way to find release.

And now I stand and wonder:
Where were you all these years?
Why did I not notice you?
And you whisper back,
I was there,
In that unexplained anxiety you so often felt.
I was there in those angry words
That escaped your lips and made you wonder where they
    came from.
I was there when you withdrew into a shell.
I was then when you laughed hysterically
To avoid a flood of tears.
I was there.
Your buried pain.
Hidden away.

But now I am free.
You have let me go.
I feel released.
I am no longer inside
Buried,
Unacknowledged.
I am released.
Free.

Now that you have let me go,
Now that you have set me free,
There is more space inside of you.
What I occupied is now open,
Open for something new.
There is space now for growth,
For new beginnings,
For hope,
For grace and compassion,
For forgiveness and freedom,
For love.
There is space now that
The walls have crumbled.
Breathe.
Be free!
I am no longer
Your
Buried pain!

Enough

It seemed to never be
Enough
Not enough time
Not enough things
Not enough adventures
Not enough gotten done in the day
Not enough days in the week
Not enough pairs of shoes – earrings – scatter cushions
Not enough of this and that
Not enough
Something inside always needed more
There was this bottomless pit in my soul
Wanting
Needing
Thinking
More – More – More
If only I had more
Then at some point it would be enough
I would be full
The empty spaces would be satisfied

But they weren't
No, the empty spaces were never filled to satisfaction
Every time I thought
This is going to fill the void
Another vacuum opened inside
Hungry to be fed
Hungry to be filled

Then one day
(How I got there I am unsure)
The hunger stopped rumbling inside
It stopped wanting – needing – to be fed
It was somehow satisfied
By that which was

Somehow it dawned on me:
Enough was around me
Enough was inside me
Enough was what is
Not what comes next
Enough is in the now

In the flower blooming in the garden
In the lyrics of a song playing on the radio
In the breath I take
In the smile I was offered
In a kind word spoken
In the raindrops falling on the ground
In the gentle wind and the stillness of the night
In the storyline of a book
In the fresh air at the end of the day
In a painting unfolding

Enough was
In a warm cup of coffee to start the day
In the rising sun
In the dawn of a new day
In the strength of family
In the depth of true friends

In the laughter of a child
In the energy of the young
In the wisdom of the old
In carrying another's load
And letting another help carry mine
In sharing life
In speaking
In listening
In being authentic and true
To myself

This was –
This is –
Enough

Healing

I long to feel whole again
I long to feel there is solid ground under my feet
I long to feel the rhythm of my heart beating steadily
I long for my thoughts to be ordered and steady
I long …
I wish ….
But it feels like the destination called wholeness
Is so out of reach
And I don't know how to get there

As I walk through the thick fog of pain
Waiting, trying, wishing
I remember your wisdom
Wisdom generations of people before me
Generations of people in pain
Have gathered and grown to understand
People who bravely, courageously
Faced their pain
And trod the path of healing

You passed their wisdom on to me
And through the fog of my mind I remember
I heard your gentle voice of wisdom
Telling me

Healing does not happen overnight
Healing takes time
Becoming whole is a journey

It's a messy road
And you need to do it
One step, one moment, one day
At a time
Mindfully
Don't rush it
Don't press fast forward
Be patient
Patient with the pain
Patient with yourself
As you experience the gravity of it all

Healing takes trust
Trust that all you feel has a place
Every experience of anger, fear, disgust, sadness
Every one of them is okay to feel
Don't judge what you feel!
And don't judge yourself for feeling
But feel what you feel!
Trust that feeling the whole spectrum
Of your human heart
Will
Slowly
In time
Bring healing.

You will ask: Why?
You may have to ask: Why?
It is human nature to ask: Why?
But remember this:
The answer to this question

Will not necessarily make the pain less
Nor will it necessarily make the journey easier
The pain you feel
Will still be painful
So, ask the question
But don't hold onto it for too long in the hope
That when you have the answer it will bring relief
It more than likely
Won't

Rest and rest
The journey of healing
May feel like you are running a marathon
Without having walked more than a hundred metres
Healing happens on the inside
Happens in your heart
Your soul
Your mind
To the outside world it is invisible
But on the inside
In the unseen places
Your energy is being sapped
To restore you to wholeness
So, remember to rest

Find a trusted person who can listen
Someone who does not need to fix it
Someone who can just sit with you
As you tell your painful story
As you give words to what you think and feel
As you speak your truth

As you express your truth
As you hear your own truth
Tell your story without judgement
Of yourself
And the messiness of it
Give it a voice
Your story needs to be told

Don't beat yourself up when you find yourself
Unable to forgive just yet
Remember: You are probably not there yet
You have not reached that place yet
But you will in time
If you want to
If you are prepared to be intentional
Remember:
Forgiveness is first and foremost about setting yourself free
Free of resentment and anger and bitterness
Carrying these into the future of your life
Will make your soul heavy
And rob you of the beauty of life
You will know when you have reached that place
When you realise this
Forgive

And then
When you can
Embrace the moments that feel
A little lighter, a little easier
Meaningful moments
Allow them to feed your soul

Allow them to give you hope
Allow them to energise you
Allow them and live them
They are important moments
To remind you that
There is life beyond the pain

As these words make their way
Through the fog
Through my pain
Reminding me of
This wisdom
Handed down for many generations
I feel I can breathe a little lighter
I will get there
I will arrive
One day
At this place called
Wholeness

I heard God's whisper ...

I look at the landscape of the world
I see so much pain and suffering
I see heartache and fear
I see anger and revenge
I see destruction and rubble
And I see midst it all
Eyes full of anxiety
Tear-streaked faces
Tired souls

How will this end?
Where is our world heading?
What future awaits us?
What lies ahead for generations to come?
These questions bounce around in my head
And they make their way into my heart
Where I begin to feel a deep sense of anxiety and dread

I can't see across time
But as one day flows into the next
I feel fear rise in my soul.

I call out to God and share my anxious thoughts
I ask Him to intervene and to bring an end to this
I plead with Him to help me make sense of it all
I pray that God somehow stops this runaway train

But I have not been able to hear Him
Through my racing thoughts
And my anxious heart

Maybe there is too much noise

And then this morning
I sat quietly
I breathed deeply and listened to the birds
As they sang their morning melody
And finally I heard a whisper

My child
The world has always been a hard place to live in
The world has always seen pain and destruction
The world has always seen hardship and hate
The world has always seen greed and a worship of power
The world has always known the song of anger and fear
It may feel new to you
But it's not new to Me.
I have known it this way from the word go
But I promise you midst it all My love has always
Dwelt amongst it!
And it continues to do so
Be still and see where love is shared between the rubble
Listen carefully for kind words spoken between the noise of
    destruction
Watch as little acts of kindness bring about relief in another's
    heart
See where meals are shared, and a hand reaches out to
    another to help cross a road

Listen to where a mother sings a song as she rocks her baby
    to sleep
Watch where people draw together and find courage and
    hope in community
Look closely
Stop and listen
There you will discover Me
I always have and still do and always will
Dwell amongst you

And when you notice this, I trust you will find courage
For the next step
The next day
I will never leave or forsake you
I will make a way
Also for your timeline
And as the whisper passes like a breeze
I open my eyes and I feel something different inside
A sense of peace that passes all understanding
My racing thoughts have stopped
My anxious heart has calmed
Maybe just for a moment
But a moment I will treasure

I remain in this place for a moment longer
And then I rise from this place
I take another step into the unknown that lies ahead
Into the future of our times
With something new inside

I heard God's whisper.

Hold onto hope!

When life is not a straight line
When the waves keep crashing
And the waters threaten to drown you
Hold onto hope
Hope that beyond the horizon there is a place
A place waiting for you where the waters are calmer
Where the lines are straighter
The waters are shallower
Hold onto hope

When the jagged pieces of your broken heart
Cut mercilessly into your fragile soul
With no regard for its vulnerability
Hold onto hope
Hope that beyond this moment
The colours of joy will one day shine
Through the cracks the rainbow will find a way in
And you will experience beauty and joy again
Hold onto hope

When the thick fog descends on your mind
When life is a blur, and you battle to see clear outlines of
    anything
Your vision is smudged, and your memory is a merciless
    sieve
Hold onto hope
Hope that the fog will lift
That clarity will return

That the disorientating mist will dissolve
Hold onto hope

When your soul asks question
When, why, how and where keep circling around it
When God seems silent and disinterested
Hold onto hope
Hope that one day
You will find peace with no answers
A peace that surpasses all understanding
And you will rest in that
Hold onto hope

When you can't see the path
And have no strength to take the next step
Hold onto hope
Hope that He has gone ahead of you
He has walked and made the path straight
He has calmed the storm and prepared a place
He has cleared the way
Hold onto hope

Hope there is life beyond the pain
Hope that one day you will reach this life
This place
Where you will live, and breathe and laugh
Again
Hold onto hope

Holy Ground

We sat together for a while
And in this space in time we shared
You opened a door
You let me in

You let me in!
You let me see the smudges on your soul
The deep sadness you still carry deep inside
About things that didn't turn out the way you so longed for
You let me listen as you spoke of shattered dreams
You let me share the depth of disillusionment
In life, in others, in yourself
And all the pain that comes with it.

You let me touch your anxious thoughts
Hear your voice that still choked
As you tried to find words to express
What was going on inside
You let me see the tear-stricken face of your past hurts
That led to the fear you carry inside
That still dictates so much of your life
You let me hold your hand as you voiced your mistrust
Of the world, of others, of those you love
Of yourself!
The things that have left a visible scar on your sense of
    worth
You let me see how deep the fear flows
Of being

Left
Forgotten
Rejected
Abandoned
Alone

You let me see
You let me touch
You let me feel
You let me hear

You let me in

When I left that shared place in time
When I walked back into my own life
I turned around for a moment
I looked back and I knew
I had just stood
On Holy Ground

I Failed ....

I failed
I fell
The gravity of my mistake pulled me
Down
Down into a dark valley with steep cliffs on either side
Down into a place from which I did not know
How to return

I lay there
In this abyss
My knees bruised
My hands scraped and bloody
From wanting to buffer the impact of
My fall
I lay there
Not able to move
Not able to rise
Not able to think
I was numb

What now?

But then I managed
Managed to slowly open my eyes
They adjusted to the darkness around me
They saw the depth I had descended into
From whom I thought I was
To whom I had become.

All I could do is
Lie still
And allow the reality I had created
Move through my numb body

The air returned to my lungs
I sat up
I began to think
How do I return from here?
I realised
Only by letting go
Letting go of that which had such a strong hold
On me

The only way out was to
Let go of
My pride
My ego
My sense of power
I had fallen
I had failed
I could not hide from this
It was what it was

As I slowly rose from to my wobbly knees
I began the hard climb
Out of my valley of desolation
Leaving behind
My determined pride
My robust ego
My solid sense of power

This was weight
I could not carry with me
From my fall
It would just hold me back

As I climbed
I knew there was only one thing
I could hope for:
Grace

Grace
Larger than myself
Stronger than my ego
More determined than my pride
More powerful than my own sense of power

I hoped
I would discover this
This grace

And I did

It shone into my heart like a bright ray of sunlight
It warmed me inside
It showed me the way
From failure to forgiveness
From the past into the future.
It was this grace
That changed me

It made me
More compassionate
More patient
More humble
More accepting of my own humanity
And the humanity of others

It was grace
That was stronger than my ego
Bigger than my pride
More powerful than power itself
It was simply
Grace

My wish for you ...

I don't wish for you a year of easy answers,
But a year where you have the courage
To delve deep and grapple with those hard questions
So that you can find answers that give rest to your soul.

Nor do I wish you a year with all the answers
But rather that you can make peace
With those that remain unanswered.
That you have moments where you experience
The profoundness of these words:
"A peace that passes all understanding".

I don't wish for you a year without self-doubt,
But that you are brave enough to unpack
Those destructive lies so deeply entrenched in your mind.
And that you discover yourself and embrace all areas
Of who you are
And that this truth will set you free.

I don't wish you a year of light and lightness,
But that you can always believe that light will follow,
That God, Who made the heavens and the earth,
Will speak over your life:
"Let there be light"
And you will discover the power hidden in these words:
"And there was".

I don't wish you a year without grief and loss,
But that in the crashing waves of your despair
You will find comfort and relief,
Strength to take the next step
And keep holding the hand of the One
Who walks on water.

I don't wish for you a year free of fear,
But that in and with the fear you do it anyway
And discover in this walk
The fountain of courage and faith that flows deep inside
    your veins.
That you embrace these words:
"Be courageous and strong for the Lord your God goes with
    you".

I don't wish you a year without conflict,
Conflict with those you love and those you don't,
But I wish for you that you will find ways, in these,
To create wholeness and healing
And uphold the God-given dignity of the other
And yourself.

I don't wish for you a year without mistakes,
But a year where you can own them,
Where you can lay down your pride
And discover the lessons to be learned
And experience God, Who loves you anyway.

I don't wish for you a year of observing life from a distance,
But a year where you embrace life with both hands,
With all its facets and paradoxes,
And in this discover your uniqueness
And what it is that you are called to bring to the world.
That you live your life trusting the One who said:
"I have come to give you life",
Life to the fullest.

I don't wish for you a year without sin,
But that in your sin you find your way back to Calvary
And that at the foot of the cross you find relief
From the burdens that lie heavy on your heart
And you discover how humility empowers you.

I don't wish for you a year where the path you walk is
    simple,
But a year where you are patient enough
To work out the uniqueness of the path you travel
And that on this journey you continue to come across
The great gifts of God's love and Grace.

I don't wish for you a year where you shed all vulnerability,
But a year where you allow yourself to be that fragile
    person,
Where you affirm your own humanity,
That you trust that in the messiness and that
Your eyes of faith are opened
To the mystery of this truth:
There is always a message in the mess.

I don't wish for you a year full of happiness,
But a year in which you discover that
The joy of the Lord is your strength.
A joy that remains, even when things around you
Are not as simple as you would like them to be.

And (maybe) most of all,

I don't wish for you a year where all your dreams come true,
But a year in which you trust that God is holding and
    moulding you
Into the perfect dream
He has for you.

I will wait for you ...

When you fall into the abyss
That deep dark place you so feared
That place of shadows
Of shame
Of buried hurts
Of imperfections
That place that is part of your truth
Not out there
But deep inside
In your heart
In your soul
In the forgotten memories

When you go there
Or fall into this place
Or are forced there by life
Know this:
I will wait for you

When you go there
Life will be rocked to its very foundation
Of what you expected
Of what gave meaning
Of what made sense
Of who you thought you are
Or thought you were
Or expected to become

When you go there
Wounds you thought long healed may burst open
Releasing a volcano of pain
Thoughts that helped you to make sense of life
May be at war with each other
May be a litany of paradoxes
And the thread that held them together
Will be thinly worn and leave you in murky waters
Choices you made with good intentions
May leave your core shivering
And make you question
Just about everything you chose
Guilt may flood into your already weary lungs
While shame may hover vividly in your dreams
Dark feelings that once were safely tucked away
May come to the surface
Leaving a blanket of despair
Heavy on your soul

But remember this:
When you go there
Or are forced to go there
I will wait for you

I will wait for you
In between
The before and after
That place of "not yet there"
When you fumble your way through
The thick mist
Of no man's land.

I will wait for you
I will wait for you
Because
You are doing a brave thing
You have gone
Where angels fear to tread to
A place where you will discover
A bigger part of who you are

I will wait for you
Because
It is on this journey that
I know you will find more wholeness
You will discover healing
You will discover more of
The valuable person
You are

I will wait for you
Because
It will make you
Softer
More compassionate
More humble
More human

I will wait for you
Because
It is here that you will find the depth of what
"My Grace is sufficient for you" means
I will wait for you

To welcome you back
When you rise from the abyss
More whole
More healed
More gracious
More you
More

I will wait for you
Patiently
I will hold this space in time for you
Quietly, gently, patiently
With hope
I will wait for you

What I ask in return
Is simply this:
When I go there (which I will)
Forced into those shadows by life
Please
Wait for me!

A shattered dream

That day
I held it in my hand
My life
My mind, my heart, my soul
My dream
All together safe in the palms of my hands
And the gentle hands of my Maker.

Then it dropped
Then it shattered
Then it lay all over the floor in
A million little pieces.

For a moment, a long moment
All I could do was stare.
There was nothing inside of me that could respond.
Midst the shattered pieces
There too lay my response.
I guess it was on the floor too
In a million little pieces!

But then the numbness left.
It lifted like a cloud,
Very slowly,
But lift it did
And exposed what lay beneath.
The sharp edges of my soul,
The bruised areas of my heart,

The splinters of my mind.
And with the lifting of the numbness cloud
Came
The piercing pain that ripped through my being!

I wanted the cloud back.
I longed for the numbness to return
But it had lifted and exposed
What could no longer be hidden.

As the pain ripped through me, I looked down at my palms
Where once I thought I was safe.
In those hands
There was now only emptiness.
And my eyes of faith search for the gentle hands of my
    Maker,
My Creator.

But those hands seemed also to have disappeared,
Vanished,
Disappeared into thin air
With the cloud of numbness.

And the pain continued to rip through my body
And I didn't know where to from here.
My hands attempted to pick up the pieces,
But every time I bent down
To pick up
The pieces of my heart, my soul, my mind,
It were as if it cut deep into my flesh
And left an open wound on my shaking hands.

The pieces of my mind began to break through
And some of my heart came alive through the bruises
And the sharp edges of my soul started to cut questions into
   me.
Where are you, God, my Creator and Maker?
Where were Your hands when it dropped?

And there was silence.

Where? Where? Where?
My bruised heart, the pieces of my mind and the sharp
   edges of my soul
Continued to cry
And my eyes expressed the pain
In a flood of tears.

And then,
Through my blurred vision
I began to see,
See the outlines of those gentle hands –
Strong, steadfast, steady,
Creator Hands –
And through my blurred vision I began to make out the
   shapes.
They had not disappeared,
They had just moved
A little lower
To catch,
To hold,
The shattered pieces
Of my dream.

Where have you come from?

I look back
Back at what was
And this question whispers into my soul:
"Where have you come from?"
And I stop for a moment today
Curiously looking back
Curious to reflect
On those moments
That have now turned into memories
Where have I come from?

My memory takes me to moments
Moments of complete exhilaration and joy
Moments filled with adventure
Moments of adrenaline rushing through my veins
I remember how I walked towards those moments
Knowing they were coming
Curious to see how the adventure would unfold
Life-giving
Energising
Fun
Joyful
Moments
Moments that blew life into my soul

But
These were not all the moments
That moved through the time-line of the past year
Into the space of memories
I remember the other days and months too!
Moments
When curiosity had no space
Not in my heart
Nor in my mind
Not in my soul
Times when
An avalanche of turmoil descended
And covered my curiosity with
Rocks and stones and mud
Of despair and hopelessness
Curiosity was missing in action
And my word became
Survival
Surviving turmoil
Surviving grief
Surviving anger
Surviving pain
Surviving fear

It is only now that I see that
I survived
Now
I can look at these moments
Curiously
To discover the deeper meaning

The lessons learned
In surviving

I recognise the hand of my God
Holding
Moulding
Comforting
Encouraging
Loving
Me
I look back at survival
And discover
The value
Of the avalanche
I survived

Where have you come from?
I search for the words
I came from the dance
Between
Despair and Hope
Laughter and Tears
Energy and Exhaustion
Light and Dark
Curiosity and Survival
That's where I have come from

Simply receive ...

I watched you that day
As you reached out
Your hands no longer steady
Your skin no longer smooth
Your body now bound to a wheelchair
But you reached out
To receive
With trembling hands
The cup of life

I saw you close your eyes
Slowly bringing this cup to your lips
Sipping
A small sip
To make sure not to choke
You took
You drank
And then, your hands still shaking,
You handed it back
This cup

I watched
I wondered
What was it, in this moment
That stirred my spirit?
You who had lived so much longer than me
You who had lived life for eighty plus years
What happened inside your soul

In this moment?

I looked again at your aging, unsteady hands
Hands that had worked hard
Hands that had held life
Hands that had built and planted
Hands that had reached out to others
Hands that had soothed a broken heart
Hands that had picked up many a fallen person
They must have been strong hands
Steadfast hands
Stable hands
In their younger years

But now they are shaking
Trembling
They can no longer heal and fix
They can no longer build and plant
They can no longer lead and guide
Age has weakened these hands
They can only reach out
And simply receive
From the cup of life

It is then that my soul grasps
The lesson in this moment
You think these hands of yours
Are too weak to teach
Anyone
Anything
Anymore

Yet they teach me this:
There comes a time in life
When we need to let go of wanting our hands
To fix, to make right, to do
There comes a time
When all our hands can do is this:
Simply
Reach out and
Receive

By your wounds I am healed

I sat across from you
You looked at me with kind gentle eyes
But my hands were clenched in tight fists
My shoulders stiff
My teeth grit together
My whole body tight with anxiety
Uncertainty
Fear

Then you began to speak
You told your story
You opened your hands
So that I could see
The remnants of old pain that still ran in your veins
The shredded pieces of doubt and fear you carried
The sharp edges of guilt carried long after the mistake was
   made
The shame that had defined so much of your life
The doubts
The unanswered questions
The un-finished story

You opened the hands that carried all of this
And so much more
You opened them for me
It all lay there
Exposed
So that I could see

See you with all that you carried
See you
Not as perfect and complete
But as someone
Who was just like me
A wounded person

The difference between us was this:
Your palms were open
My hands, on the other hand, were
In tight fists
Afraid of what would happen
If I opened them
And showed you
What was cutting into the palms of my hands

I looked at you
Your eyes remained
Full of kindness
Full of compassion
And your hands
Remained open
So that I could see your wounds.

Something unexpected happened in this moment
I felt the tension ebb out of my shoulders
I felt my heartbeat slowing down
I felt my hands no longer in tight fists
But slowly able to open up
Only a little
But open they did

In this moment I began to feel something new inside
I felt hope that I too could survive the wounds I carried
I felt relief that I was not alone in my struggle through life
I felt hope that I too could reach a place that felt more
    whole

You showed me your hands that held suffering and pain
It was in your exposed struggles
I found relief
I found hope

It was through your wounds
That I began
To heal

The End

It is seldom that I think about you
THE END
You seem very far away
You seem so out of reach
Somewhere behind the distant horizon
Far away from my now
I live as if you will never be reached
I live with lists of things I can do tomorrow
I will call tomorrow
I will make peace maybe later
I will ask how my friend is doing next week
When life stops being so busy
Then
I will

Because the END is still far away

Then something happens
And the END knocks on my door
It wakes me up to this reality
The END will come
I don't know when
I don't know how
I don't know where
But it will make its away into my present

Because
The END will not wait forever
Time in this life
My time
My parents' time
My friends' and family's time
Is limited
It has an expiry date
It will
One day
Not knock on my door
But it will simply break in
And meet me where I am
And say
I am here

The END

As I ponder this truth
As I reflect on this moment
My heart flutters a little
As the reality of this wakens my senses
I do not have control over this moment
I do not know when or how or where
It will meet me.

I don't know when it will come

THE END

But as I move towards it
I realise I have a choice
I can choose
I can choose how I want to live
I can choose to embrace every day as a gift from God
I can choose to be kind and encouraging towards others
I can choose to be patient with those who test me
I can choose to be honest with others and myself
I can choose to celebrate special moments
I can choose to love those who come across my path
I can choose to heal myself so that I don't bleed over others
I can choose to be light in a dark world
I can choose life now
I can choose
A life-giving Life

Till
THE END

About the Author

Elke grew up in a small town, Greytown, in the heart of Kwazulu-Natal. She attended Hermannsburg school and completed her matric in 1990. After this, she spent a year au-pairing in Germany, before starting her studies at the University of Pietermaritzburg, where she studied for her Bachelor in Theology. During this time, she was offered an opportunity to live in Tanzania for six months. She returned home from this adventure, completed her degree and did an internship in Namibia and Cologne, Germany, respectively, for a year in each place. She then worked as a school chaplain for three years in Hermannsburg, went on to run an NGO in Pietermaritzburg for seven years, where her focus was on supporting vulnerable children and families in poor communities. It was an amazing time in her life, being able to live and work so close to the realities of the divide between rich and poor in our country.

Thirteen years ago, she moved to Winterton in the Drakensberg with her son David, where she now the pastors the Winterton Lutheran Congregation. She says: "I have pastored the church here and learned a great deal of the 'human struggle', a continuation of my work days in the NGO sector." While pastoring the church she did some further studying with the Victor Frankl Institute, which gave her a deeper insight into Frankl's life, the search for meaning in life and the humanity we all carry inside.

She says: "During my working life I have walked alongside the very rich and the very poor: a vast spectrum of people. It has given me insight into life, and the struggles that people face in their daily realities. Poverty can have many faces. As Mother Theresa says, 'The hunger of love is always much harder to remove than the hunger for bread'. Regardless of where we find ourselves in life, we are all in search of love, acceptance, understanding and encouragement. I hope that this book encourages a wide range of readers to find hope, see love, accept the journey of life and trust that life is good and God means well with His creation."